Original title:
Pulsar Poetry

Copyright © 2025 Creative Arts Management OÜ
All rights reserved.

Author: Maya Livingston
ISBN HARDBACK: 978-1-80567-784-0
ISBN PAPERBACK: 978-1-80567-905-9

Harmonics of the Cosmos

Stars hum tunes in the night,
While planets dance with delight.
With each jiggle and spin,
Nebulas chuckle, let's begin!

Comets tailgate in style,
Asteroids grin all the while.
Black holes keep the secret stash,
While quasars flash a cosmic flash!

Celestial Beamings

In the Milky Way's disco ball,
Shooting stars rise for a ball.
Galaxies twist, they want to groove,
With cosmic beats, they keep the move.

Saturn wears a ring so tight,
Jupiter's storms are quite the sight.
Uranus gives a sideways glance,
While Mars winks, ready to dance!

Timeless Frequencies

Time ticks in a galactic dance,
Gravity pulls, but stars take a chance.
Neutrinos giggle as they slide,
While photons race, full of pride.

Light-years pass with such flair,
The universe's tale is beyond compare.
Singularity's spin gives us a thrill,
Bringing laughter with a cosmic chill!

Resonance of the Skies

The sky chuckles with stars so bright,
Echoing laughter through the night.
Meteor showers rain down giggles,
As starlit whispers create jiggly wiggles.

Celestial beings toss jokes 'round,
In constellations, humor's found.
Galactic pranks with playful grins,
As the cosmic show of fun begins!

Light Pulse Symphony

In the dance of photons, they twirl and spin,
Like disco balls grinning, they beckon us in.
With strobe-light giggles, they jump through the night,
Making shadows giggle, oh what a sight!

The rhythms of cosmos, it tickles the mind,
They bounce and they bounce, leaving logic behind.
A waltz of wavelengths, it's all rather bright,
Where light's just a jokester, with puns of pure light.

Celestial Musings

Up in the heavens, where stars flash a grin,
They chuckle at comets that tumble and spin.
Space junk's got the humor, a laugh at our plight,
As planets play tag in the endless twilight.

With Saturn's rings jiggling, oh what a tease,
While Mercury zips in and out with such ease.
A cosmic ballpark, where laughs are the game,
With Martians in bleachers, who all know your name.

Beyond the Event Horizon

What happens to jokes that fall in the hole?
They stretch into laughter, but lose all control.
The punchline's a mystery, a giggle gone dark,
As black holes are laughing, it's quite the remark.

Where gravity's joking, with a tug and a tease,
It pulls in your giggles; try laughing if you please!
Einstein's got humor, in folds of the space,
With wrinkles of joy, that curve time's funny face.

Gravity's Embrace

In the arms of gravity, we wobble and shake,
As if we're all marbles on a cosmic lake.
With every attraction, a chuckle ensues,
When orbits collide, it's just some good news.

Falling for laughter is what we do best,
We tumble and spin, forgetting the rest.
As the universe giggles, pulling us near,
We float in the fun, wrapped in cosmic cheer.

Echoes of the Universe

In space where all the giggles roam,
Stars play tag, they call it home.
A comet trips, its tail a mess,
The moon just laughs, in a moonlit dress.

Black holes spin a wild joke,
While asteroids dance, a cosmic poke.
Aliens chuckle, with tentacles wide,
As they zoom by on a starlit ride.

Lightwave Lullabies

Shooting stars sing a tune so bright,
While Saturn's rings hold a disco night.
Galaxies spin, holding in their mirth,
Creating ripples all over the earth.

Nebulas puff, a colorful plume,
As planets gather for a dance in gloom.
Lightyears apart but still so near,
They share a laugh, filled with cheer.

Cosmic Sonnet

Venus winks, with cheeky delight,
While Mars flexes, ready to fight.
Stars play soccer in the dark,
Kicking light beams, oh what a lark!

Asteroids laugh with a thudding sound,
As they bounce in space, round and round.
Comets wear hats made of stardust,
Who knew space could be so robust?

Pulsing Starfields

In fields of stars where laughter glows,
Celestial bees buzz while the humor flows.
Wormholes open with a goofy grin,
Inviting all for a wild spin.

Quasars beam with a chuckle so grand,
While planets gather to make a band.
Galactic jokes travel lightyears wide,
In this comic dance, they all abide.

Constellation Chronicles

In the void where stars play tricks,
A comet sneezes, and it flicks.
The moon rolls dice, it's quite absurd,
While planets dance without a word.

Galaxies giggle, light years away,
Sending jokes in the Milky Way.
Asteroids chuckle, what a sight,
As black holes hide in the dark of night.

Ethereal Beats

Beats from space, a funky tune,
Neptune, spin your hula hoop soon.
Jupiter's jiggle, a wobbly twist,
While Saturn's rings give a cosmic list.

Dancing debris, what a parade,
Shooting stars in a wacky charade.
A meteor mash-up, oh what a ball,
In the rhythm of the night, we all enthrall.

Orbiting Sonnets

Venus sings to a squirrel above,
While Earth spins tales of a wayward dove.
Mars invites all with a pie in the face,
Comets crash in a floury race.

Satelites skit, they twirl and glide,
Asteroids tease, it's a wild ride.
In the dance of the orbs, hilarity reigns,
With laughter echoing through cosmic plains.

Celestial Cadence

Stars twinkle like they're taking a bow,
While space rocks wear hats, oh wow!
Nebulas giggle in colors so bright,
As black holes whisper, 'We'll party all night.'

A stardust shuffle, a wormhole swing,
Galactic laughter is the best thing.
With playful comets chasing a kite,
The universe hums in pure delight.

Afterglow and Starlight

In the afterglow, I trip on a star,
Wishing I could dance, not dance so bizarre.
With twinkling lights that giggle and wink,
I slip on a comet, oh what do you think?

Jokes in the cosmos, laughter in space,
Even the moons have a grin on their face.
Saturn spins tales of rings that confound,
While I just bounce like a ball on the ground.

Sonic Constellations

Stars hum a tune, a cosmic delight,
A saxophone asteroid making the night.
Planets are jamming to beats from afar,
While asteroids mix it up in a bar.

The Milky Way's band plays, it's quite a sight,
With meteors drumming, oh what a fright!
Galaxies swirling in a playful chase,
But I just got lost in the deep space embrace.

Dances of Light

Flashes of brilliance waltz through the dark,
Light beams do cartwheels, oh what a lark!
Colors are swirling like candy on cheer,
While shadows just giggle, they've nothing to fear.

A conga line forms on the edge of the void,
Where even black holes feel slightly annoyed.
The starlit ballet, it's all quite a show,
But watch where you step, or you might lose a toe!

Rhythm of the Spheres

Spheres spin and twirl in a cosmic ballet,
While I try to boogie, but slip on my sway.
Gravity's pulling, but I'm feeling quite free,
Just a clumsy old star, laughing at me.

The beat of the universe echoes and swells,
With planets all laughing, they sparkle their spells.
I trip on a needle of light shining bright,
As meteors chuckle, they say, 'What a sight!'

Quasar Dreams

In a galaxy far, far away,
Stars giggle and play all day.
Comets racing, they can't be late,
Shooting beans on a cosmic plate.

Aliens dance in a silvery light,
Socks on their heads, what a sight!
They twirl and spin with great delight,
Who knew space could feel so bright?

Asteroids bounce, like a funfair ride,
Gravity's weird, they won't abide.
Planets spin with a joyful glide,
Join the party, it's open wide!

Nebulas laugh, colors collide,
Painting the skies with stellar pride.
Each quasar's wink, a cosmic guide,
To dreams where humor won't subside.

Interstellar Serenade

A tune from a star, oh what a sound,
Where black holes dance round and round.
With a pluck of a comet, a chord gets struck,
It's a cosmic joke, just our luck!

Shooting stars drift on a breeze,
They whisper punchlines with such ease.
Floating through space, we take the tease,
Life's too short, let's laugh and please!

Space whales sing in harmonic waves,
While moonbeams bounce, the silence saves.
Galactic giggles, what fun they pave,
Life in the universe—wild and brave!

Drifting in rhythm, we sway and swing,
With each star's twinkle, we laugh and cling.
Shooting our dreams on this cosmic spring,
Interstellar joy is our forever thing.

Echoes of Infinity

In the depths of time, a joke resounds,
While galaxies spin, laughter abounds.
Echoes of giggles in the void,
Even black holes can't help but be coy!

Silly wavelengths bounce and they play,
Riding space winds in a carefree way.
Quarks and leptons, what fun they say,
Join the symphony, come what may!

Cosmic rays burst with laughter loud,
Even the cosmos feels so proud.
Milky Ways swirling, a shimmering crowd,
Tickling our fancies from every cloud.

Time loops giggle, twisting our fate,
In this vast expanse, don't hesitate.
Join the laughter as we oscillate,
Echoes of joy that won't abate.

Radiant Rhythms

Stars drum on the beats of the night,
With meteors dancing, oh what a sight!
Galaxies waltz, in rhythm take flight,
A cosmic party filled with delight.

Each pulsating color, a playful jest,
The universe pokes us, it knows us best.
Gravity's pull is no time to rest,
Join in the fun—come be our guest!

As planets jiggle and moons do the twist,
In this stellar circus, you can't be missed.
Fun in the void, oh what a tryst,
With radiant rhythms, the cosmos kissed.

So let's paint the night with laughter and cheer,
In this boundless realm, where dreams appear.
With every heartbeat, we boldly steer,
Creating memories, adventures dear.

Astronomy of Emotion

In the cosmos of giggles, we float,
Stars giggle brightly, on a cosmic boat.
Planets spinning tales of woe,
While comets laugh, all aglow.

Asteroids throw parties, wild and bright,
Dancing in orbits, a hilarious sight.
Even black holes, in their deep despair,
Crack jokes about losing all their hair.

Nebulas blush in shades of pink,
Making faces, with a wink.
Galaxies swirl in a humorous waltz,
Creating memes of cosmic faults.

In this sky of jokes, we all appear,
Finding laughter, year after year.

Harmonic Expanse

In the vastness, a symphony plays,
Stars laugh softly, in funny ways.
Waves of giggles ripple through space,
Echoing joy in the wide embrace.

Saturn's rings, a great clown's hat,
Jupiter spins with a gleeful pat.
Mercury zips with a buzz so fast,
Calling all planets to join the blast.

Cosmic choirs sing in a breeze,
Meteorites tumble, all with ease.
Each twinkle a chuckle, bright and free,
Harmony floats through infinity.

We dance among planets, friends and foes,
Sharing the laughter, as stardust flows.

Universe Unwritten

In a blank space, where stories hide,
The stars scribble tales with cosmic pride.
Jokes in the dark, waiting to unfold,
Each quasar chuckles, brave and bold.

Time bends here, in a playful twist,
Gravity giggles, it can't resist.
Space and laughter collide with glee,
Writing the universe, just you and me.

Dark matter jumps in, tries to play,
Hiding behind stars, all night and day.
Its silent jokes, just out of sight,
Keeping us laughing till morning light.

With comets trailing tails of fun,
Every story told, a cosmic pun.

Radiance of Reflection

Light beams bounce in a joyful spree,
Reflecting smiles for all to see.
Galactic mirrors, polished bright,
Show off the chuckles in the night.

In this kaleidoscope of glee,
Sunlight dresses the world in spree.
Every beam a silly thought,
In laughter's light, we all are caught.

Reflections twist, like humor's way,
Bouncing back laughs at the end of the day.
Each photon dances with a wink,
In the laughter that makes us think.

So gaze upon this gleeful show,
Where each reflection helps joy grow.

Brilliance in Motion

Stars twinkle like a disco ball,
Dancing lights in a cosmic hall.
Planets shuffle to a funky beat,
Groovin' through the stellar street.

Gravity's got moves, so sly and neat,
You can't resist a celestial tweet.
Comets swing with tails so bright,
Making wishes feel so light!

Asteroids join in the cosmic fun,
Rolling and tumbling, they can't be outdone.
Galaxies spin like a whirlpool dive,
Twinkling bright, oh how they thrive!

Space is a party without a doubt,
Where laughter and stars do spin about.
In this dance, joy takes its flight,
As we twirl through the velvet night.

Orbiting Dreams

In a world where planets wear sunglasses,
They strut their stuff with such pizzazz.
Moons parade in shiny attire,
While shooting stars ignite the fire.

Fleets of rockets race and zoom,
Creating a raucous cosmic boom.
Nebulas swirl in a cotton candy hue,
As dreams orbit on a cosmic skew.

Meteor showers rain down laughs,
As stardust fills our goofy drafts.
Astro-puns and cosmic cheer,
Bring the universe to our sphere.

Galactic giggles echo around,
In the humor of space, joy is found.
So let your dreams take flight so high,
In this stellar show, we can't deny!

Sonic Nebula

In a nebula painted with sound,
Cosmic giggles bounce all around.
Echoes of laughter form a tune,
Bouncing off asteroids like a balloon.

Whirling stars play hide and seek,
Winking at planets with a cheeky peek.
Rockets whistle a merry hymn,
While comets jive on a galactic whim.

Through space, the jokes fly fast,
Making even black holes laugh at last.
Harmony drips like cosmic cheese,
As waves of fun bounce with ease.

In this sonic field of light,
Astros chuckle with pure delight.
Let's turn the universe into a playground,
Where laughter and starry dreams abound!

Stellar Pulses

Stellar pulses make a quirky beat,
Like a solar flare doing the shuffle feat.
Galaxies hum a silly song,
And cosmic critters dance along.

Stars throw a light bulb flicker,
Twirling like a cosmic sticker.
Wrinkled rags of asteroids sway,
While meteors act out their play.

Every pulse is like a giggle burst,
In the cosmos where joy is first.
Celestial shenanigans drown all fear,
A universe filled with laughter and cheer!

So let's skip through moons and rings of gas,
Chasing dreams as we laugh and pass.
With stellar pulses in our stride,
We'll dance through the cosmos, side by side!

Rhythm of the Cosmos

Stars twinkle in their dance,
Planets wobble at a glance.
Cosmic giggles fill the air,
Gravity pulls our funny hair.

Space dust tickles all night long,
Asteroids hum a silly song.
Aliens laugh like it's a joke,
In a universe where we're all woke.

Light-years stretch like a rubber band,
Galaxies prance, a merry band.
Black holes burp with a loud cheer,
What a strange way to steer clear!

Supernovae burst with flair,
While comets whip up cosmic hair.
The universe spins, what a hoot,
In this cosmic jig, who needs a suit?

Nebula's Song

In the clouds of colorful light,
Stars are born, it's quite a sight.
Nebulae giggle, swirl and spin,
Creating colors where dreams begin.

Dust bunnies floating, stirring cheer,
Comets pop in, give a sneer.
Planets munch on cosmic pies,
Who knew space had such sweet fries?

Galactic whispers, bold and sly,
Meteor showers, oh my, oh my!
Asteroids waltz, with a clumsy twirl,
While stardust flakes around them swirl.

Laughter echoes, a cosmic tease,
With every flicker, it aims to please.
Nebula's song is a playful tune,
In the vast expanse, we dance under the moon.

Galactic Heartbeat

In the heart of the galaxy's beat,
Wormholes wiggle, it's hard to seat.
Stars pulse with a comical thump,
While space critters gather and jump.

Asteroids rolling, slippery ride,
Jokes and pranks at every side.
A black hole winks, then gives a shove,
Who knew dark matter could giggle with love?

Galaxies spinning in comic flare,
With supernovae bouncing everywhere.
Quasars chuckle, a distant sound,
In this cosmic circus, joy abounds.

Stars in pajamas, ready to nap,
Floating on dreams, taking a slapp.
Cosmic heartbeat, a funny tune,
In the vast universe, we sway 'neath the moon.

Cosmic Verses

In the void, a joke takes flight,
Stars laugh at the speed of light.
Comets dance with glee and flair,
While planets join in, without a care.

Astro-bunnies hop in delight,
Shooting stars zoom out of sight.
Galactic giggles echo wide,
In this space, there's nothing to hide.

Superheroes made of stardust spin,
In a universe, absurd but akin.
Meteorites tumble with a sound,
As cosmic wonders abound all around.

With each verse, the cosmos plays,
A melody of the silliest ways.
Through the void, let laughter roam,
In the universe, we've found a home.

Orbiting David's Stars

In the dark, David spins with glee,
His quirky stars dance like a bee.
Each one twirls with a silly grin,
They giggle as they orbit and spin.

A comet with a dazzling tail,
Sings karaoke, oh what a tale!
Saturn's rings all clink and chime,
As asteroids rhyme for the umpteenth time.

David juggles meteors with flair,
While aliens stop, and openly stare.
Black holes give a playful shout,
As starry laughter echoes about.

Celestial Harmonies

The moon strums chords on a cosmic lute,
While stars kick back in their starry suit.
Jupiter hums a jolly tune,
Pluto sneaks snacks, making good use of the moon.

Neptune's got bubbles that tickle and fizz,
While Mars cracks jokes about starry whiz.
Galaxies swirl in a cha-cha beat,
Silly stardust dances on cosmic feet.

The Milky Way giggles, twinkling bright,
As comets perform in the spacey night.
Laughing lights form a chorus line,
In a universe full of quirks divine.

Through the Cosmic Lens

A telescope winks with mischief and cheer,
While telescopes gossip, 'Did you see that deer?'
Planets peek through with a secretive glance,
All eager to join in the cosmic dance.

Asteroids wear hats made of glitter,
Stars go "zap"—but never do quitters.
Galactic selfies with Martian fluff,
Every snapshot is goofy and rough.

Coming together, they hold a great show,
Winking bright like it's their own cabaret glow.
Through the lens, the universe teases,
Crafting jokes that bring cosmic breezes.

Constellation Imprints

Orion's belt is made of old socks,
And Ursa Major wears wooden blocks.
Twirling, they mark the starry skies,
With talented stars that all improvise.

Sirius barks, it's a starry dog,
Making fun of a synchronized fog.
While Cassiopeia blows bubbles in air,
Pisces swims by without a care.

Together they form a humorous tale,
Crafting laughter with each cosmic sail.
Imprints of charm in a stellar display,
As the universe giggles in its own way.

Nebulae Narratives

In a cloud of fluff, stars said, "Hey!"
They bounced around, bright and gay.
One tripped on dust, shouted, "Gloober!"
And space laughed hard, the grand old trooper.

Galaxies danced in a swirl of cheer,
While comets cracked jokes, oh so clear.
A quasar winked, "What do you call it?"
A giggle so loud, it made space a bit hot.

Supernovae burst with surprise, oh so bright,
Said, "Did you hear? Stars come out at night!"
Stardust sprinkled all over the scene,
Echoing laughter, the best ever seen.

In the backdrop dark, they swirled and spun,
Where humor lives, and no one's outdone.
In the vastness, jokes echoed loud and clear,
As each cosmic light shared a chuckle, sincere.

A Symphony across Space

Planets whirled in a merry dance,
Bumping around, they took a chance.
One said, "Oh, let's play hide and seek!"
But the sun just spun, lighting up the week.

Asteroids clinked like silly bells,
Each collision told tales, no one repels.
"I'm the rock star!" one proudly cried,
While meteors laughed, swishing by with pride.

Saturn's rings grooved, what a sight,
Twisting and turning, full of delight.
"Hey, let's jam with a cosmic beat!"
As stars clapped along, got up on their feet.

In this feast of fun, all were invited,
Where laughter and whimsy were ebullient, unblighted.
A concert of joy, far and wide,
With every twinkling note—on humor's ride.

Cosmic Heartstrings

Stars strummed strings as they twinkled so bright,
Each melody playing under the night.
"Hey Moon, you shine, why don't you croon?"
She giggled back, "Maybe after noon!"

Black holes teased, "What's your favorite snack?"
Nebulas chuckled, swirling in a pack.
"I like dust bunnies, like Taffy and Fuzz!"
"Oh please, dear friend, that's part of the buzz!"

Planets shipped jokes in a cosmic belt,
Each punchline shared, all warmly felt.
A comet zoomed past, with a wink and a grin,
"Told you, space parties are where we begin!"

Thus laughter echoed through the stellar night,
Binding all together in sheer delight.
A symphony played, sweet and absurd,
As hearts danced wildly, never deterred.

Lyrical Lightbends

Light beams stretched, forming a smile,
They jiggled and danced in cosmic style.
"Twinkle like us, don't you see?"
Every wink said, "Join the spree!"

Space-time warped with a giggle and swish,
From planets and stars, a grand, silly wish.
"How do you catch a moody star?"
Light replied with a bow, "Just click 'an' it far!"

In a realm where the absurdity reigns,
Each lighthearted joke creates the chains.
Stardust sings right in cosmic hues,
Every shimmer spins tales, bright and profuse.

So join the fun, let your laughter soar,
In the spins and twirls of the cosmic lore.
For even in darkness, joy lights the bends,
Creating music where even light descends.

Pulsing Stardust

Twinkling lights in a dance,
They jiggle and swirl with a glance.
Stars wear hats and funny shoes,
In this cosmic party, it's hard to lose.

Galactic squirrels play tag at night,
While moonbeams giggle, oh what a sight!
Asteroids bounce like rubber balls,
Their playful chaos breaks down the walls.

Nebulas twist in a silly style,
Doing the cha-cha, oh what a while!
Black holes spin like ballerina socks,
Making time wobble like a chicken pox.

Comets slide with a whoopee cushion,
Creating laughter, a cosmic confusion.
In this stardust realm so bright,
We dance and giggle till morning light.

Orion's Lullaby

The hunter snores with sparkling dreams,
His belt jiggles, or so it seems.
Stars sing softly, a soothing tune,
As meteors race, chasing the moon.

Sirius winks, a cheeky light,
Whispering jokes that spark delight.
Andromeda giggles, hair in a whirl,
While Milky Way twirls in a cosmic swirl.

A cosmic cat naps on Mars,
Dreaming of chasing playful stars.
Galaxies swirl in a whimsical spin,
While black holes chuckle—let the fun begin!

Orion snores, but the stars don't care,
They toss confetti across the air.
In this lullaby, where giggles bound,
The universe sings in hilarious sound.

Twilight Frequencies

Crickets chirp in cosmic sync,
While stars sip tea and giggle, I think.
The moon plays fetch with little clouds,
As fluffy jokes build up in shrouds.

Constellations whisper cheeky puns,
While shooting stars race just for fun.
Orbs of laughter, swirling about,
In this twilight, joy makes us shout.

Waves of laughter ripple through the night,
As planets gather, all feeling bright.
Jupiter juggles, rings all aglow,
While Venus teases, "Come on, let's go!"

In this hazy glow of twilight's gleam,
Reality bends; it's all a dream.
Jump in the fun; don't miss the chance,
In this cosmic jam, come join the dance!

Cosmic Paradox

In a galaxy where socks go lost,
Twinkle-toed aliens dance at any cost.
Stars mix up colors—green, blue, and red,
Forget the weather; it's all in your head.

Planets play hopscotch in zero gravity,
While gravity giggles with madness and levity.
Time takes sidesteps, just for the heck,
As clocks dance circles around your neck.

Black holes belch with a cosmic laugh,
As stardust falls like confetti from a staff.
Supernovae throw parties, oh what a sight,
Balloons and punch—an interstellar night!

In this paradox where fun meets the grand,
The universe unfolds—oh, isn't it grand?
Join the song of the stars, take a spin,
In this cosmic conundrum, let joy begin!

Pulsing Galaxy Ballads

In the void, stars play tricks,
They wink and giggle, quite the mix.
Galaxies swirl in a cosmic swirl,
Twinkling bright like a happy girl.

Comets race in a swooping flight,
Chasing shadows through the night.
A black hole belches, oh what a sight!
It swallows starlight with pure delight.

Nebulas fluff like cotton candy,
While planets dance, oh so dandy.
Aliens laughing in their spacey way,
Throwing a party for Milky Way.

Asteroids take a tumble, and roll,
Creating chaos, that's their goal.
But in the end, they giggle with glee,
In this cosmic jest, all are carefree.

Stellar Stanzas

In the depths of the starry sea,
A supernova sings with glee.
Meteorites juggling, look at them go,
They're the best comedians in the cosmic show.

A quasar cracks a pun so bright,
It lights up the darkness, what a sight!
Planets spin in a dizzy parade,
While space dust twirls, unafraid.

Galactic giggles echo around,
As starlit jokes bounce, profound.
Orbiting moons share tales of jest,
In this vast universe, they find their rest.

With a wink and nod, they take their space,
Floating in joy, they share their grace.
So here's to the cosmos, full of cheer,
In the laugh of the stars, we find our sphere.

Void's Ballad

In the empty void, echoes of cheer,
Where shadows flicker, and jokes appear.
Ghostly stars whisper funny fears,
Tickling space-time with cosmic sneers.

Empty space, but not quite bare,
A galaxy dance, with quirky flair.
Black holes chuckle, spinning around,
Devouring light, making it confound.

A neutron star snores like a bear,
While asteroids practice their dance in pairs.
Scattered laughter, a cosmic jest,
In the boundless void, they're all truly blessed.

Planets prance in a merry line,
Juggling laughter as if divine.
In this vast emptiness, joy takes flight,
In the heart of the void, there's always light.

The Dance of Lightyears

Across the cosmos, they sashay and swing,
Stars tap dance, what a sight to bring!
Lightyears twinkling, flashing bright,
In a galactic dance party, oh what a night!

Galaxies tango, their arms entwined,
Laughter echoes in the space they find.
Nova pops confetti, a brilliant display,
Celebrate with comets, hip-hip-hooray!

Supernova spins, it steals the scene,
While space dust glitters, oh so serene.
In the ballet of orbs, so eccentric and wide,
The universe holds its laughter with pride.

So let's join in this stellar spree,
Joke with a nebula, dance carefree!
For in the dance of lightyears so bright,
We find that even galaxies delight.

The Silence of Stars

In the night, stars giggle,
Tickling the dark, oh so fickle.
They twinkle with laughter in light,
Whispering secrets of cosmic delight.

Asteroids dance with comical flair,
Shooting past like they haven't a care.
Each planet serves jokes on a ring,
Gravity's pull is a playful fling.

Maybe UFOs are just shy,
Hiding behind clouds that float by.
Aliens laugh at our silly ways,
While we count stars on endless days.

The silence between them is a jest,
Making us ponder, perhaps in jest.
Under the moon, we chuckle and muse,
While the stars giggle, just for our views.

Time's Lightplay

Tick-tock goes the cosmic clock,
But what if it just likes to mock?
Light beams racing, a cosmic chase,
Time's a comedian, full of grace.

Moments stretch like spaghetti lines,
Turning minutes into funny designs.
Chronos twirls in a jester's cap,
While we get lost in the humor trap.

Seconds flip like pancakes round,
Falling onto laughter's sweet ground.
Light plays tricks behind our backs,
Sneaking a peek, before it cracks.

Walking the timeline, I trip and fall,
Time rolls like a ball, what a brawl!
In the end, we all have a say,
Light just laughs as we sway and play.

Lyricism of the Skies

Clouds jot down verses in the air,
Each puff a word, without a care.
They float like poets, frolicking free,
In the sunlight's spotlight, full of glee.

Rain taps gently, a rhythm divine,
Nature's beat, oh so benign.
Thunder chuckles with a mighty roar,
While lightning scribbles on skies to score.

The wind, a bard, sings of the day,
Spinning tales in a breezy way.
Nighttime's curtain draws up tight,
Stars drop verses, twinkling with might.

Here in the vastness, they play and rhyme,
What a funny dance, lost in time!
From horizon to horizon, no one is shy,
The lyricism of skies makes us all sigh.

Echoing Between Galaxies

In the void, echoes take the stage,
Witty words, they dance and engage.
Galaxies giggle, their laughter rings,
As they nudge each other with silly flings.

Comets arrive with a burst of cheer,
Hopping across space, they disappear.
Their trails write jokes on a cosmic scroll,
While black holes swallow them whole, oh what a stroll!

Sound waves tickle, they bounce and roam,
Between the stars, they find a home.
With each laugh, the cosmos expands,
Creating more room for all our plans.

So let's shout out to the dark's delight,
For humor's a star that shines ever bright.
In the vastness where echoes resound,
Laughter and joy are beautifully found.

Celestial Cadence

In the sky, a dance of dots,
Twinkling bright, like hula spots.
Stars giggle in a cosmic whirl,
A silly galaxy, watch it twirl!

Comets zoom with flashy tails,
Whispering jokes on solar sails.
Planets wobble with a grin,
Inviting all to join the spin!

Saturn's rings, a hula hoop,
While Venus twirls in a cheerful troop.
Mars tells tales of ancient pranks,
As stardust swirls in cosmic banks!

So raise a toast to stellar fun,
In this universe, we dance and run.
Laughter echoes through the night,
In this grand ball of galactic light!

Frequencies of Night

The moon hums tunes of silly dreams,
Crickets croon in starry themes.
A bat swings by with a perfect dive,
Singing songs only night can thrive.

Jupiter jokes with its stormy might,
While Pluto grumbles, "I'm still in sight!"
The cosmos laughs at comical sight,
As shooting stars burst with delight.

Asteroids dance like quirky kids,
In a playground made of cosmic grids.
Galaxies swirl while stardust giggles,
In this ballet of cosmic wiggles!

So tune your ears to the night's delight,
For laughter echoes through the infinite light.
Each frequency a tickle of joys untold,
In the vastness where fun never gets old.

Astral Reverberations

Neon stars with funky beats,
Make the universe tap its feet.
Cosmic rhythms in a grand parade,
Where every quasar's a serenade!

Black holes joke about being dense,
While shooting stars dance in suspense.
Galactic winds go whoosh and sway,
As comets join the fray in play!

Starlit laughter fills the void,
With every twinkle, we're overjoyed.
Cosmic confetti in every flash,
As planets giggle and stars all clash!

So listen close to the astral cheer,
In the silence, joy's quite clear.
The reverberations of the sky,
Make you chuckle and wonder why!

Galactic Beats

In the cosmos, an upbeat sound,
Where rhythm and fun abound.
Stars strut in their shiny coats,
Playing tunes on cosmic boats!

Nebulae swirl in pastel hues,
Grooving to the galaxy's blues.
Planets bop with silly grace,
As the universe picks up the pace!

Asteroids roll like happy clowns,
In their playful cosmic gowns.
Hyperspace zones twist and bend,
Where every loop brings joy, my friend!

So dance along to the galactic show,
Let your spirit and laughter flow.
In this wide expanse, take your seat,
For the grandest of all cosmic beats!

Whirls of the Universe

In a galaxy far, stars do spin,
Chasing their tails, they think it's a win.
Planets hold dance-offs, oh what a sight,
Jupiter's lost, but he's feeling all right.

Comets with popcorn, they zoom and they glide,
Asteroids chuckle, they take it in stride.
The Moon cracks jokes, and the Sun's got style,
Even black holes smile, though they're hard to rile.

Nebulae giggle, they swirl about,
In this cosmic circus, there's no room for doubt.
Stars throw confetti, cosmic drips everywhere,
Who knew the universe had so much flair?

Gravity pulls, but it's a game of tag,
Stars dart and dodge, they're never a drag.
The cosmos winks, in its playful parade,
Laughing with stardust, in the starlit glade.

Timeless Echoes

Waves of laughter ripple through space,
Whispers of stars with a grin on their face.
Light years away, they still find their glee,
Sharing old tales, as bright as can be.

A cosmic clatter, oh what a sound,
In the infinite void, where jokes can rebound.
Echoes of giggles bounce off the blink,
Galactic puns making everyone think.

Comets draw mustaches, the moons roll their eyes,
While meteors race, winning first place in the skies.
Time flies, but the jesters hold tight,
In this timeless show, there's no end to delight.

Every supernova bursts into cheer,
Confetti of stardust, oh what a sphere!
Distances shrink when laughter's the call,
In this comedy club, there's joy for us all.

Wavelengths of Wonder

Radio waves dance, with jitters and shakes,
Sending out signals, oh what fun it makes!
Wavelengths twist, in a cosmic charade,
Every quirk and quibble, a grand masquerade.

Giggles from quasars, sparking delight,
Whirling in cycles, oh what a sight!
Frequency floods, where the humor runs deep,
In this vacuum of jokes, the starlings leap.

Light shows and punchlines, they all intertwine,
In rhythms of laughter, oh how they shine!
Starlight's the spotlight, actors take stage,
The universe chuckles, no need for a wage.

Howling at voids, and winking at black,
Stars trade their secrets, they're never off track.
In this cosmic comedy, let's cheer and play,
Wavelengths of wonder, our dreams on display.

Cosmic Poetry in Motion

Planets whirling in their cosmic dance,
Each step a giggle, a twirl, a prance.
Space-time's a jester, with endless tricks,
In this cosmic ballet, we're all in the mix.

Saturn's rings blush with giggly delight,
While Venus wears shades, saying, "Hey, that's bright!"
Galaxy's gossip travels far and wide,
As comets laugh hard, in their shimmering ride.

Orbits collide, with a twist or a loop,
Planets exchange jokes in their merry troupe.
The void sparkles with a mischievous grin,
A universe chuckling, let the fun begin!

Asteroids juggling, in a space-bound fair,
Each moment a punchline, rare and fair.
In this motion of cosmos, we float and jest,
Cosmic poetry flows, it's simply the best!

Nebula's Heart

In the sky, a dance we see,
Stars wobbling so joyfully.
A cosmic twirl, a stellar prance,
Even asteroids join the dance!

With comets zipping, tails so bright,
They tickle planets late at night.
Galaxies bounce in merry spin,
While black holes grin and pull us in!

Supernovae bursting into cheer,
Making neighbors disappear.
While gas clouds giggle, twist, and swirl,
Creating chaos in a twirl!

Oh, Nebula, with colors wild,
You light up space, so free and styled.
Join in laughter with every flare,
In cosmic corners, joys we share!

Intergalactic Musicals

A show in space, oh what a sight,
Singing stars, oh so polite!
With moons tap-dancing on their beams,
Performing splendid cosmic dreams!

Asteroids form a rock band crew,
Playing hits like "Space is New!"
With meteors jamming all night long,
Filling the void with their funny songs!

Planets sway in a charming line,
While Saturn spins in a grand design.
Mercury taps on cosmic keys,
Bringing laughter with galactic ease!

Galactic jazz, it fills the air,
With gravity's waltz, we sway and share.
In this show of stellar delight,
Every note twinkles, oh what a night!

Eternal Starlight

In the night, a star so bright,
Winks at us, oh such delight!
A thousand years, it shines, it winks,
Filling dreams with cosmic links!

Yet somehow, they're always late,
For light-years may just complicate.
"Hello?" we shout, they giggle back,
"Still waiting on our light attack!"

A galaxy promises it'll beam,
But truth be told, it's just a dream.
While time plays tricks, we wave and cheer,
Eternal starlight, always near!

Underneath the cosmic show,
We laugh out loud, all aglow.
For even in this vast expanse,
Stars remind us to take a chance!

Echoing Through the Void

In the void, we hear a sound,
Giggles of the lost, unbound.
Echoes bouncing off the walls,
Laughter from the cosmic halls!

"Is anyone there?" we often call,
Only to hear a bit of squall.
Yet, from the silence comes a sigh,
"Just us space-folk, waving hi!"

The quiet chuckles, soft and dear,
Lie drifting on the atmosphere.
With whispers shared across the sky,
Cosmic jokes that never die!

So here we float, in fun delight,
With echoes making space so bright.
Through the void, the giggles fly,
In this funny cosmic high!

Waves in the Cosmic Sea

In a sea of stars, I surf and glide,
My board's a comet, what a wild ride!
Aliens laugh as I wipe out,
Floating by, 'Is that a fish?' they shout!

Galaxies twirl like a cosmic dance,
I trip on stardust, not taking my chance.
Moonbeams laugh as I tumble away,
Sending my snacks to another Milky Way!

Black holes giggle, they just can't wait,
To gulp down my chips—it's a cosmic fate!
Celestial tides pull me here and there,
But with a laugh, I embrace the cosmic air.

In the waves of the night, I'm a cosmic clown,
With cosmic jellybeans, I'll never frown!
Each star a joke, a twinkling tease,
In the universe's chuckles, I find my ease.

Quantum Serenades

In the world of quirks, I can't be late,
A dance in an atom, it feels first-rate.
Schrodinger's cat just rolled its eyes,
'Late to the party? Oh, what a surprise!'

With particles hopping like they own the show,
I try to keep track—this way, that way they go!
Entanglement's crazy, it ties me in knots,
When I try to explain, my friends just laugh lots.

I sing to my quarks, they wiggle and sway,
Light as a feather, they come out to play.
In a realm where weird is just the norm,
I find joy in chaos—it's a quantum storm!

So bring on the laughter, let fun be the guide,
In this tiny world, I take every stride.
When the universe giggles, I can't help but beam,
In these quantum serenades, I dance and I dream.

Starfall Lyrics

Stars tumble down like clumsy friends,
Each one a wish that never quite ends.
I catch one in my hat, it's a bit too bright,
'Excuse me, my friend, you're out of sight!'

Meteor showers with all their flair,
Pelt me with giggles, floating in air.
I dodge and I weave, a starry ballet,
Tripping on starlight—oh, what a display!

With cosmic confetti, the night does parade,
Galaxy giggles in a shimmering cascade.
In the laughter of space, I find my delight,
With each falling star, I dance through the night.

So let's toast to the fun, as stars hit the ground,
Wishing for laughter when silliness is found.
Through the vastness of night, I make my own tune,
As the universe chuckles beneath the full moon.

Metaphors in the Milky Way

In the Milky Way, metaphors play,
Each star a line in a silly ballet.
I pen cosmic rhymes with a twinkle and cheer,
In this galactic circus, there's nothing to fear.

Nebulas puff, looking like clouds of cream,
While light-years pass by in a giggling dream.
A black hole grins, 'You can't escape me!'
But I chuckle back, 'I'm a quantum bee.'

Planets gossip as they spin around,
Sharing old jokes they've in orbit found.
Saturn giggles, its rings all a-blur,
While Venus sings songs that make Mars concur.

So let's float and frolic in this starry expanse,
Where laughter's the rhythm and joy is the dance.
With metaphors spinning and cosmos aglow,
In the Milky Way's humor, it's fun to just go!

Lightyears of Verses

In a spaceship made of cheese,
My cat's the captain, so at ease.
We zoom past stars, oh what a sight,
She swats at comets, day and night.

Space snacks float, we munch and munch,
Galactic grapes, a cosmic crunch.
Planets giggle, twinkle and twirl,
While my cat's chasing a space squirrel.

Aliens wave from their green glow,
They think we're strange, but we just flow.
We dance on rings of Saturn's size,
With laughter echoing through the skies.

But when we land, in nebula dust,
I swear that cat can't be trusted!
She steals my snacks and steals the show,
Oh, space adventures, what a glow!

Galactic Whispers

Stars gossip softly, in silver threads,
While I ponder life on planet beds.
My socks are missing, where could they be?
The Milky Way holds them, just wait and see!

Rocket mice zoom past my head,
With helmets on, they dance instead.
They twirl and swoosh near crystal ponds,
It's hard to focus on cosmic fronds.

I trip over stardust, oh dear me,
The universe plays tricks, can't you see?
A black hole's laughter fills the void,
As I chase my dreams, somewhat paranoid.

Yet with each giggle from the skies,
There's joy and wonder in all the sighs.
So I'll pack my tales, all brightly wrapped,
And share them 'round the cosmos, zapped!

Luminous Stanzas

Dancing beams of light, what a show,
I scribble lines as they ebb and flow.
Asteroids laugh with a rolling spin,
While my coffee cup has a loose pin.

Shooting stars with funky styles,
Winking at me with goofy smiles.
I reach for one, fall flat on my face,
A cosmic blooper, oh what a grace!

Space-time giggles as I complain,
Why does the universe drive me insane?
But every stumble becomes a rhyme,
Luminous tales through the fabric of time.

Now I float in this wobbly rhyme,
With glowing words, I dance with time.
The cosmos chuckles, a brilliant spark,
In these luminous stanzas, I leave my mark!

Interstellar Cadence

In the quiet hum of the cosmic night,
My socks converse, such a silly sight.
With stars as the audience, they sway,
As I trip on stardust in disarray.

Napping comets sneak by in haste,
Creating a dreamy, celestial space.
I ask, "Are we lost?" They just twinkle,
A rhythm of laughter, in silence they crinkle.

Rocket ships sing with a cheerful tune,
Swirling around like a cosmic swoon.
Each note a wink from the universe wide,
While I try to play, my giggles collide.

As I float on this interstellar beat,
I gather the whimsy, the joys to repeat.
Each silly moment a lyric I find,
In the cadence of stardust, laughter defined!

Luminous Frequencies

In the night sky, I saw a light,
Saying, "Hey there, I'm quite bright!"
Flashing signals after dark,
In my heart, it left a spark.

Dancing beams in endless space,
Like disco lights in a cosmic race.
Twinkling jokes from distant stars,
Making memes with Martian cars.

They beam their laughter, just for fun,
Joking 'bout how time is none.
Winking at planets with glee,
Orbiting humor, oh so free!

When I feel down in my small town,
I look up and can't help but frown.
Those luminous spheres, so far away,
Make my worries just fade away.

Stellar Reverie

Oh, the stars have quite the sense,
Of humor that's most intense.
They chuckle from their lofty heights,
Throwing jokes like shooting lights.

In a cosmic cafe, they gather round,
Swapping tales with a chuckle sound.
Sipping space tea, dreaming bold,
Sharing stories of galaxies old.

One star once said, "Earth's really weird!"
As comets burst, and laughter cheered.
With every twinkle, wink, and grin,
The universe laughs and spins.

So float along in this stellar glee,
With cosmos humor setting you free.
Join the dance, let your spirit soar,
In this brilliant nebula, forevermore!

Aurora's Dance

The Auroras twist and twirl in flight,
In colors that make day seem bright.
They giggle and glide, putting on a show,
Like ribbons of laughter in the snow.

"What's the mood?" the north winds tease,
"Let's dance with colors, swirl like leaves!"
With every shimmer and every sway,
They play with night, come what may.

Pinks and greens and shades of blue,
Creating a ballet, all brand new.
As they prance across the chill,
The world beneath can't help but thrill.

So join the ball, in this sky so grand,
With every step, take a chance, take a stand.
Up in the heavens, where fun knows no end,
The night laughs back, a jovial friend!

Lightyears of Lament

A star once sighed from a far-off place,
"Oh dear, what a slow galactic race!"
Lightyears away, the punchline's spare,
Yet shadows linger, everywhere.

It spoke of comets, with wistful cheer,
"We chase our tails, year after year.
While planets spin, we yawn and joke,
In the vastness, we still invoke.

But asteroids wander, bumping about,
Creating chaos in their route.
With tiresome thoughts of cosmic sorrow,
A queasy universe waits for tomorrow.

Yet within the gaps, humor untold,
Shines through darkness, brave and bold.
In lightyears of lament, we find delight,
As stars unleash their laughter into the night!

Beyond the Lightyear

In a spaceship made of pizza,
We zoom through the galaxy's glee,
Past planets with pets and candy,
It's a cosmic jamboree!

The stars are our disco lights,
We dance with aliens in shoes,
They tell the worst dad jokes,
While we all just hum the blues.

Comets chase us with their tails,
Shooting past with a sparkling grin,
They say our laughter fills the void,
But really, it's the cheese we spin.

Let's toast to space-time shenanigans,
With fizzy drinks in our hands,
In the universe's vast playground,
Where silliness forever stands.

Celestial Resonance

The moons sing silly ballads,
In harmony with starry night,
Their giggles echo through the void,
As they polish beams of light.

Asteroids throw a rock concert,
With meteors dancing around,
They'll jam till they run out of breath,
Then pretend they never found.

Galaxies spin in crazy hair,
As comets join the parade,
With trails of glitter and sparkles,
Who knew space could be so staged?

We'll grab some stardust smoothies,
And toast with laughter anew,
In this realm of cosmic antics,
Where joy is the best debut.

Dreaming Among the Stars

I dreamed of a cow on a rocket,
Mooing tunes from outer space,
She jumped over the moon for laughs,
In her sparkly, starry grace.

With Martians who juggle planets,
And nebulae spinning in bliss,
They formed a band of nerdy stars,
Playing tunes we can't dismiss.

Chasing the sun's vibrant rays,
We tumbled through cosmic fun,
Falling into each other's arms,
While whispering secrets on the run.

Let's twirl 'round Saturn's rings,
And waltz on Jupiter's face,
In a dreamland of laughter,
We'll dance till we leave a trace.

Spectrum of Silhouettes

A cosmic game of hide and seek,
Planets peek behind the sun,
With shadows casting silly shapes,
Making everyone laugh and run.

The black holes pull pranks with flair,
Swallowing socks and fun toys,
While stars gossip about the dark,
Creating colorful space noise.

In a nebula's wacky fashion,
We play dress-up with light and shade,
Creating outfits that sparkle bright,
In this cosmic masquerade.

Let's ride the waves of laughter,
As orbits twirl in delight,
In the spectrum of silhouettes,
Where joy thrives through the night.

Radiant Connections

In the vastness of space, I found a mate,
A star with a wink, oh it's not too late.
We dance through the cosmos, with laughter so bright,
Our photons collide, what a comical sight.

Galaxies giggle, as we zoom on by,
Taking selfies with comets, aiming high.
I told Orion a joke, he laughed 'til he shone,
A chuckle in starlight, we're never alone.

Orbiting Words

I wrote a poem that took flight,
It looped around Mars, what a hilarious sight!
Words spinning like planets, oh what a chase,
Each stanza a comet, in this vast space race.

Venus chimed in, with a giggle or two,
Said, "Your rhymes are like asteroids, all over the view!"
We bounced off each quasar, traded puns and quips,
Creating a galaxy with laughter and flips.

Celestial Echoes

An echo of laughter from a black hole came,
Who knew space could be such a funny game?
I asked a neutron star for a light on my path,
It flashed me a grin, gave a cosmic half-laugh.

With each silly ripple, the universe swayed,
We played cosmic charades, in the starlight parade.
Jupiter joined in, with a spin and a twirl,
His stormy adventures sent us into a whirl.

Starlight Whispers

In whispers of starlight, I heard a loud joke,
From a space-loving alien with a quirky poke.
"Why did the comet break up with the star?"
"Because it needed more space, it traveled too far!"

I chuckled so hard, I fell from my seat,
Orbiting laughter, oh what a treat!
With each glowing smile across the night sky,
We light up the cosmos, laughing oh my!

www.ingramcontent.com/pod-product-compliance
Lightning Source LLC
Chambersburg PA
CBHW070751220426
43209CB00083B/400